52-WEEK
CHRISTIAN COUPLES
JOURNAL

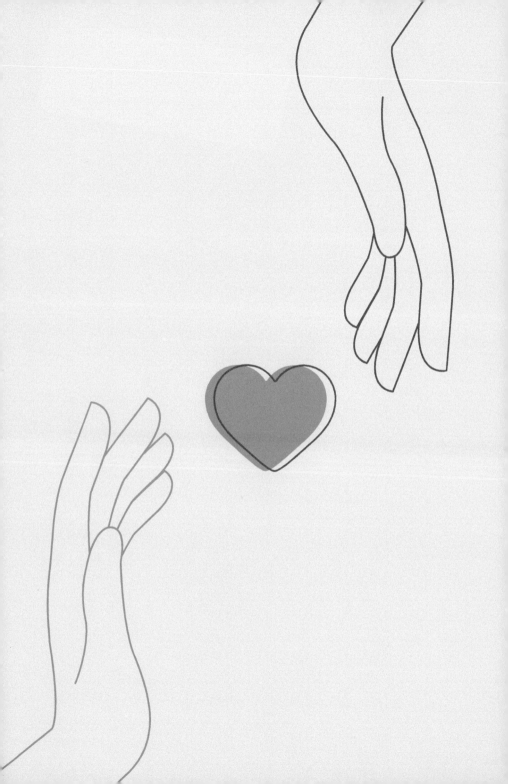

52-WEEK
CHRISTIAN
COUPLES
JOURNAL

Prompts and
Prayers to
Strengthen Your
Relationship
with Each Other
and Your Faith

JENNA GREER

**ROCKRIDGE
PRESS**

First Rockridge Press trade paperback edition 2022

Rockridge Press and the Rockridge Press logo are trademarks or registered trademarks of Callisto Media Inc. and/or its affiliates in the United States and other countries and may not be used without written permission.

For general information on our other products and services, please contact our Customer Care Department within the United States at (866) 744-2665, or outside the United States at (510) 253-0500.

Paperback ISBN: 978-1-68539-354-0

Manufactured in the United States of America

Interior and Cover Designer: Sean Doyle
Art Producer: Sue Bischofberger
Editor: Chloe Moffett
Production Editor: Caroline Flanagan
Production Manager: Holly Haydash

Illustrations used under license from shutterstock.com

10 9 8 7 6 5 4 3 2 1 0

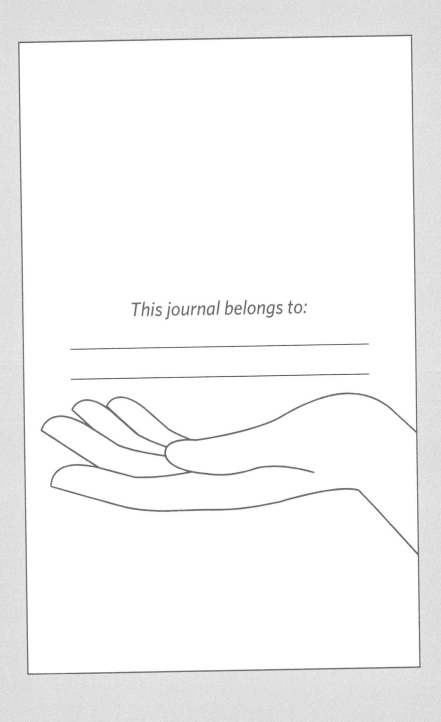

This journal belongs to:

Introduction

For as long as I can remember, I have chased after Jesus. I seek to learn more about who He is and why He paid the price He did so I could live eternally with Him. The more I dive into His Word and spend time soaking up His presence, the more I become overwhelmed by the relentless, everlasting love He has for each one of us.

Learning new ways that I could experience Jesus has become something of a habit, whether that be inviting Him in on my quiet drive, writing down prayers and thoughts that would forever be kept between the two of us, or blasting worship music so loud it drowns out any other thing taking up space in my mind. I always found, and continue to find, new ways to seek Him in my day-to-day life. One of those ways I seem to return to time and time again: journaling. There is no right or wrong way to do it, but it's always left me feeling closer to Him. On my bedside table, you can always find a journal, or multiple if you just take a quick walk throughout my home. There is something so powerful about jotting down a word you felt Jesus placed on your heart, or a quick prayer that you couldn't let leave your mind without being put to paper. Journaling is what you make it, and what you make it has the ability to be a powerful tool in opening up the presence of Jesus.

When I was just twelve years old, a seventh grader, I met my husband. I didn't know it at the time, but just four short years later, we would begin our dating relationship that led us to where we are now—married, with our second baby on the way. Throughout our relationship, we've learned to grow in faith, as individuals and as partners in life. One of these ways is journaling. Setting aside time during your busy lives to sit with your partner and seek Jesus together is one of the most powerful things you can do to grow closer to each other and keep Jesus at the center. I pray that this *52-Week Christian Couples Journal* can help you strengthen your faith, make a habit of seeking Jesus together, and experience the good things He has in store for the two of you.

How to Use This Book

In this 52-week journal, you'll find a weekly Bible verse, followed by prompts that will spark engaging conversation with your partner. There is space for you to write down your thoughts and key points from your discussions. At the end of each entry, there's a guided prayer or action of the week for you to follow along with, to help you grow closer to each other with a focus on fostering your faith walk.

This journal is meant to be done with your partner bit by bit, not requiring large amounts of time, but whenever you find a few moments to sit together. Don't worry about busy schedules—you can work through this journal whenever you have spare time and your partner by your side.

The Bible verses that you will read each week are taken from the NIV translation of the Bible. Feel free to use whichever translation of the Bible you feel most connected to or understand best. I am hopeful that this journal will be a powerful stepping-stone in your relationship with your partner and with Christ, with the main goal being that after these 52 weeks, you set forth feeling enriched in both your personal faith walk and with each other.

Week 1

And over all these put on love, which binds everything together in perfect harmony.

—Colossians 3:14

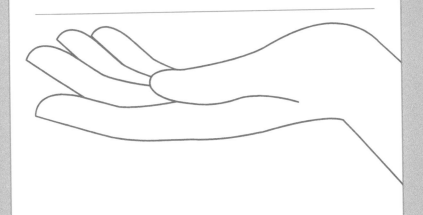

This week, pay close attention to how you include love in daily inter-actions with your partner. Being intentional in what you do and how you speak can have a great impact on the closeness you feel to your partner. Write down a few simple ways you can show your partner you love and appreciate them. Get creative with it.

PARTNER 1: _____

_____

_____

_____

_____

_____

PARTNER 2: _____

_____

_____

_____

_____

_____

Think about times when you didn't necessarily feel connected to your partner. Maybe this was due to a disagreement, hardship, or rough patch within your relationship. Did you have to make a more conscious effort to show love to them? Or did you not show love at all? If so, write down why it's important to always choose your partner, even when it doesn't always feel easy.

PARTNER 1: _____

_____

_____

_____

_____

PARTNER 2: _____

_____

_____

_____

_____

Guided Prayer

Thank you, Jesus, for Your example of perfect, everlasting love. You continually teach us that Your love is not conditional, and You show us how we can learn to better love each other. Continue to show us how we can be more intentional in keeping love as the focus in our marriage, as love is what binds us together. Amen.

Week 2

Be kind to and compassionate to one another, forgiving each other, just as in Christ God forgave you.

—Ephesians 4:32

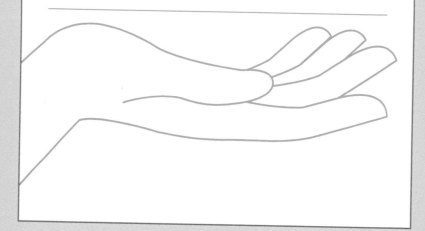

In every relationship, there will be disagreements and arguments that try to come between you and your partner. Continuing communication is vital to avoid division. Would you say that you are quick to communicate and offer forgiveness when tough situations arise? If not, what keeps you from this? How could you improve?

PARTNER 1: _____

_____

_____

_____

_____

_____

PARTNER 2: _____

_____

_____

_____

_____

_____

Think about a phrase you could say when tensions are rising in a conversation with your partner. Maybe it's something funny, like an inside joke. Or an endearment to remind the other that the love is always there. This buzzword could potentially prevent an argument and remind each other that you're on the same team. What phrase(s) can you think of? How might this strategy help you?

PARTNER 1: _____

_____

_____

_____

PARTNER 2: _____

_____

_____

_____

Action of the Week
In any love relationship, it's important to recognize the need for support: from your partner, trusted friends, and God Himself. Chat about how you can make use of outside support to strengthen your marriage. Maybe that looks like accepting a babysitting offer, if you have kids, so you can enjoy a needed date night, or asking an established couple what they've done to keep their partnership thriving year after year.

Week 3

The Lord is compassionate and gracious, slow to anger, abounding in love.

—Psalm 103:8

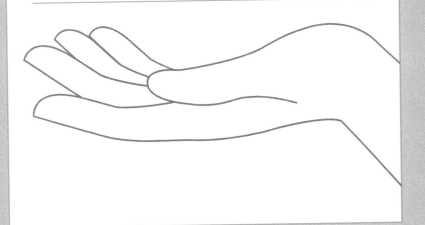

Being patient can be tough, and it takes practice to respond to certain situations with patience rather than anger or frustration. Think of a time when you noticed you were being impatient with your partner. How did you react? Did your reaction have an effect on them? What did it teach you?

PARTNER 1: _____

_____

_____

_____

_____

_____

PARTNER 2: _____

_____

_____

_____

_____

_____

Think back to the start of your relationship, when you were just beginning to learn about each other. It can be easier to walk in patience when you remember that God created you to do things differently. Talk about a time when you had to be patient, either to allow your partner to grow in a certain way or for them to open up to you about something. Describe how it felt when they became comfortable with opening up to you. Write your thoughts.

PARTNER 1: _____

_____

_____

_____

_____

PARTNER 2: _____

_____

_____

_____

_____

Guided Prayer
Lord, I am grateful that I am able to learn from You how to be more patient and understanding. Your example is laid out before me so I can practice how to first chase after understanding and gentleness, rather than jump to anger or annoyance. Amen.

Week 4

I praise you because I am fearfully and wonderfully made; your works are wonderful, I know that full well.

—Psalm 139:14

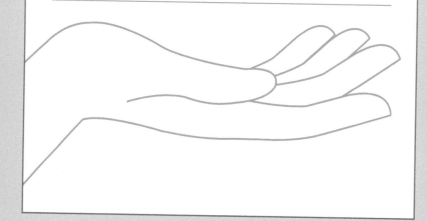

A relationship cannot flourish without love. This does not only mean love for our partner; it's also important to love who God created us to be as individuals. Think of a time when you were insecure in yourself, and your partner was able to encourage you in recognizing that the way God created you is worth celebrating.

PARTNER 1: _____

_____

_____

_____

_____

_____

PARTNER 2: _____

_____

_____

_____

_____

_____

As a relationship grows, you learn little things about each other and begin to fall in love with some of the small details. Take a couple of minutes to celebrate those details about your partner that make them who they are. List three details or characteristics your partner has and how you see God in each. (Example: *Your inviting spirit reminds me of how Jesus made it a point to be sure everyone was always included.*)

PARTNER 1: _____

_____

_____

_____

_____

PARTNER 2: _____

_____

_____

_____

_____

Action of the Week

Life is full of celebrations, big and small, that bring us joy. Even in the mundane and everyday, it's important to find time to celebrate. Make a dessert together this week. It can be as simple as cookies or brownies. Find a night that you will sit down and enjoy your dessert together as you celebrate and talk about all of the wins, big and small, from the week.

Week 5

A heart at peace gives life to the body, but envy rots the bones.

—Proverbs 14:30

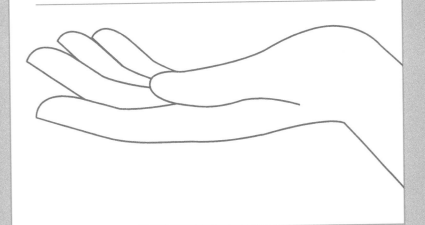

Jealousy is strong. It has the ability to take control of the mind, body, and heart. Jealousy sets out to destroy and makes it impossible to function as our best selves. Think about a time when you felt jealous. How were you able to sit back and reevaluate in order to regain your peace? What wisdom did you take from this?

PARTNER 1: _____

_____

_____

_____

_____

_____

PARTNER 2: _____

_____

_____

_____

_____

_____

Learning how to cope with different feelings, both by yourself and with your partner, can help strengthen your relationship and create a deeper mutual understanding. Discuss how you might face overwhelming feelings of envy or discouragement, and how you believe your partner could help you overcome those feelings.

PARTNER 1: _____

_____

_____

_____

_____

PARTNER 2: _____

_____

_____

_____

_____

Guided Prayer
Thank you, Jesus, for continually transforming and renewing our hearts. You show us how to lead from a place of peace rather than negativity. I am grateful that with Your help, I am able to overcome the feelings You did not intend for me to carry. Amen.

Week 6

Therefore encourage one another and build each other up, just as in fact you are doing.

—1 Thessalonians 5:11

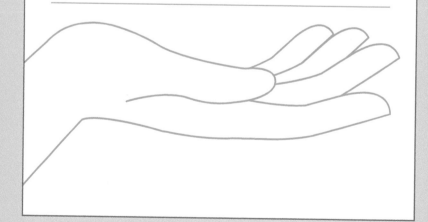

The words we say and the way we say them have a tremendous impact on each other and have the ability to make or break someone's day. It's important that we speak with purpose, with intent to encourage, uplift, or celebrate our partner. Take a couple of minutes and each take a turn giving a thoughtful compliment to the other. How does giving make you feel? Receiving?

PARTNER 1: _____

_____

_____

_____

_____

_____

PARTNER 2: _____

_____

_____

_____

_____

_____

Reflect on a time when you felt appreciated by your partner. Perhaps this was due to a few words of encouragement or a sweet gesture. Do you feel you excel at intentionally showing appreciation to your partner, or is this an area that could use improvement? Have fun discussing how your partner's appreciation makes you feel and brainstorm ways you could show appreciation toward each other.

PARTNER 1: _____

_____

_____

_____

PARTNER 2: _____

_____

_____

_____

Action of the Week

As time goes by in your relationship, it can be easy to let small, simple gestures fall out of habit. We may forget to wish our partner a good day or stop picking up their favorite treat while at the store. This week, show your partner some appreciation— it can be as simple as sending them a sweet message in the middle of the day.

Week 7

In all your ways submit to Him, and He will make your paths straight.

—Proverbs 3:6

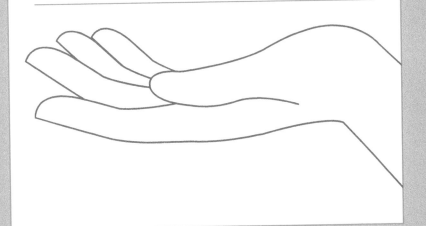

At times, we will come face-to-face with things that feel discouraging or leave us feeling confused and lost. One of the ways we can help our partner walk through something they are struggling with is by pointing them to Jesus. How can you encourage your partner to seek Jesus when they're faced with a difficult situation?

PARTNER 1: _____

_____

_____

_____

_____

_____

PARTNER 2: _____

_____

_____

_____

_____

_____

Think of a time when you struggled with something and wish, in retrospect, that you had brought it to Jesus. Share this memory with your partner, and tell them when this was, how it made you feel to face it alone, and how, looking back, you were able to see God's hand in it.

PARTNER 1: _____

_____

_____

_____

_____

PARTNER 2: _____

_____

_____

_____

_____

Guided Prayer
Lord, I am grateful that You walk with me through the situations I don't necessarily want to be in. There is no circumstance or situation in which You will leave me stranded or without guidance. Knowing that You are always with me gives me such peace. Amen.

Week 8

Do nothing out of selfish ambition or vain conceit. Rather, in humility value others above yourselves, not looking to your own interests but each of you to the interests of others.

—Philippians 2:3–4

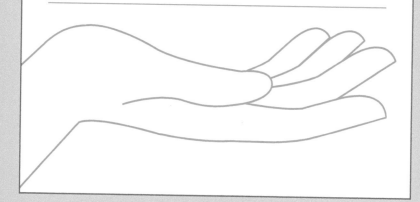

There may be moments when we want to do what feels best for us but don't take into account the feelings of our partner. We're called to be aware of what our partner needs. This week, write about how you can better serve your partner and how your partner can better serve you.

PARTNER 1: _____

_____

_____

_____

_____

_____

PARTNER 2: _____

_____

_____

_____

_____

_____

Let's chat about how it feels to have your interests made a priority. Maybe this is being surprised with a coffee on an off day or being asked to choose the movie for movie night. Take turns sharing your favorite way to be served and honored. How would you say your relationship strengthens when a point is made to honor each other's interests, both through giving and receiving?

PARTNER 1: _____

_____

_____

_____

_____

PARTNER 2: _____

_____

_____

_____

_____

Action of the Week
The Bible makes us aware of how important it is to be selfless and to first seek out how we can serve others. Set aside time this week to do something together that the other enjoys, or to try out new activities that both of you have been wanting to do.

Week 9

Therefore each of you must put off falsehood and speak truthfully to your neighbor, for we are all members of one body.

—Ephesians 4:25

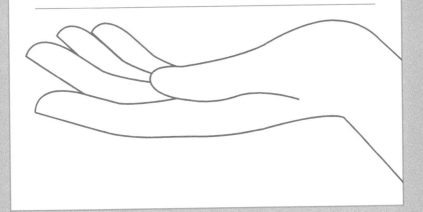

Telling the truth is important, especially within a relationship. Trust and comfort grow where there is openness and honesty. Open up to each other about a time when choosing to be honest was difficult and how the truth might have ultimately helped the situation.

PARTNER 1: _____

_____

_____

_____

_____

_____

PARTNER 2: _____

_____

_____

_____

_____

_____

Choosing honesty in times when we'd rather be dishonest is a way of humbling ourselves before each other and the Lord, and giving in to what's right rather than what feels easy. When you're faced with a tough conversation within your relationship, how can you encourage yourself to handle it with honesty and grace?

PARTNER 1: _____

_____

_____

_____

_____

PARTNER 2: _____

_____

_____

_____

_____

Guided Prayer

Thank you, Jesus. I am grateful that in times of growth and learning, You are beside me each step of the way. You want nothing but the best for me, even when what's best doesn't feel easy. You want to see me succeed in all that I do, including how I portray myself through my actions and my words. Your goodness is overflowing and Your faithfulness unwavering. Amen.

Week 10

I have told you this so that my joy may be in you and that your joy may be complete.

—John 15:11

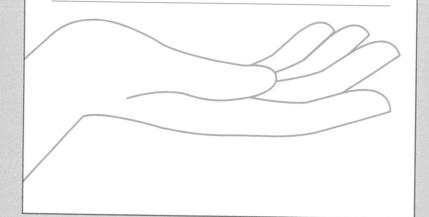

Fullness of joy comes from God. Of course, your partner also has the ability to give you happiness, but they are not fully responsible for your joy—that comes from the Lord. Discuss with your partner if this is something you have a mutual understanding on. How can you find, and encourage each other to find, joy in living for Jesus?

PARTNER 1: _____

_____

_____

_____

_____

_____

PARTNER 2: _____

_____

_____

_____

_____

_____

The joy of the Lord lives within us; it's fully accessible at all times. It's up to us to receive it and choose to walk in it. In life, there are things that set out to steal our joy and circumstances that seem to make choosing joy hard. What are things you can do to remind yourselves to choose joy, both as individuals and as a couple, even when it may be hard?

PARTNER 1: _____

_____

_____

_____

_____

PARTNER 2: _____

_____

_____

_____

_____

Action of the Week
Life is full of a bunch of little moments that make up the big ones. Let's focus on choosing joy this week, especially in the little things. Find ways to celebrate each day, whether it's going for a walk together (even in the rain) or toasting to a completed home or work project.

Week 11

Be sure to fear the Lord and serve Him faithfully with all your heart; consider what great things He has done for you.

—1 Samuel 12:24

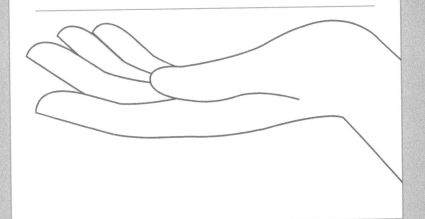

As Christians, we are called to serve God, with our hearts and our time, and in our day-to-day actions, by intentionally including Him in our day and offering help to others. Brainstorm some ways you can serve God together. Taking the time to serve others with your partner will bring you closer together and keep God at the center.

PARTNER 1: _____

_____

_____

_____

_____

_____

PARTNER 2: _____

_____

_____

_____

_____

_____

It's important that we serve God, but also that we serve our partner. Doing so shifts the focus away from a "me" attitude. Serving your partner may look like picking up a chore that they usually take care of, surprising them with a treat, or taking part in an activity they love doing. Discuss ways you can serve each other and how this can become a more frequent occurrence.

PARTNER 1: _____

_____

_____

_____

_____

PARTNER 2: _____

_____

_____

_____

_____

Guided Prayer
Lord, Your goodness is abundant; there is never a shortage. Thank You for continually improving and stretching me in ways I didn't know that I needed. I pray that I can continue to improve my heart posture to be one of selflessness, joy, and a serving heart. Amen.

Week 12

Whatever you do, work at it with all your heart, as working for the Lord, not for human masters.

—Colossians 3:23

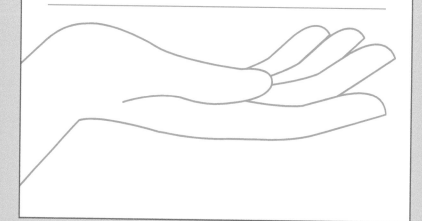

It can be easy to forget that in our work lives, we are actually working for the Lord, not other people. Forgetting who our true boss is can allow us to become disheartened. We can be each other's cheerleader in this area by reminding our partner who they are serving with their daily work. How can you encourage each other to stay focused on working with a giving spirit?

PARTNER 1: _____

_____

_____

_____

_____

_____

PARTNER 2: _____

_____

_____

_____

_____

_____

Aside from our job or career, a healthy relationship also takes a form of work. This work requires love, learning, serving, and investing in each other. At times, it may feel easy; other times, more difficult. In what ways does investing in your partner feel enjoyable to you? What are some of your favorite things to do for each other and why?

PARTNER 1: _____

_____

_____

_____

_____

PARTNER 2: _____

_____

_____

_____

_____

Action of the Week
Take a couple of minutes to sit down with your partner and write a prayer about working together to maintain a loving and flourishing relationship that pleases the Lord. Take a moment to pray your prayer over each other.

Week 13

Two are better than one, because they have a good return for their labor: If either of them falls down, one can help the other up.

—Ecclesiastes 4:9–10

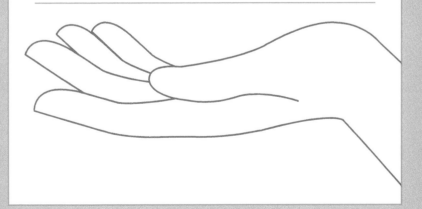

Being in a relationship also makes you a team. You're there to cheer each other on, lift each other up in times of hardship, and celebrate the wins. Discuss with your partner what you think makes a good teammate. Take turns telling each other a few ways that you appreciate their support.

PARTNER 1: _____

_____

_____

_____

_____

_____

PARTNER 2: _____

_____

_____

_____

_____

_____

Sometimes we don't realize the power our words and actions truly hold. Being supportive and cognizant of our partner's needs helps cement our connection. Take turns explaining what you believe makes you and your partner a good team in life.

PARTNER 1: _____

_____

_____

_____

_____

PARTNER 2: _____

_____

_____

_____

_____

Guided Prayer
Thank you, Lord, for placing people in our life to walk alongside us and cheer us on. We're grateful that You are our biggest cheerleader. We are amazed that the Creator of this world wants to see us succeed. You are so good. Amen.

Week 14

Trust in the Lord with all your heart and lean not on your own understanding.

—Proverbs 3:5

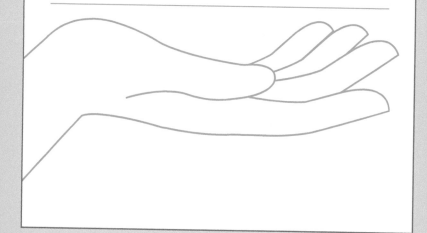

We don't have all the answers, and that's okay. Think about a difficult or complicated situation you found yourself in as a couple. How did you work together to release control and find peace, or how could you have, looking back? How do you complement each other in these kinds of times?

PARTNER 1: _____

_____

_____

_____

_____

_____

PARTNER 2: _____

_____

_____

_____

_____

_____

Learning to accept that we don't always have to know the "why" can be difficult, but it's also a blessing. The good news is that we can lean into Jesus, knowing that He has everything under control, even when we can't see it. Reflect on an area in your life, or as a couple, where you would like to become better at "giving it up to God." How could this improve things?

PARTNER 1: _____

_____

_____

_____

_____

PARTNER 2: _____

_____

_____

_____

_____

Action of the Week
In times when you don't see the "why" for what you are walking through, lean in closer to Jesus. Your partner can be of great support in this. Send each other a message of encouragement sometime this week to remind them that Jesus—and you—are alongside them in their day.

Week 15

For the Spirit God gave us does not make us timid, but gives us power, love and self-discipline.

—2 Timothy 1:7

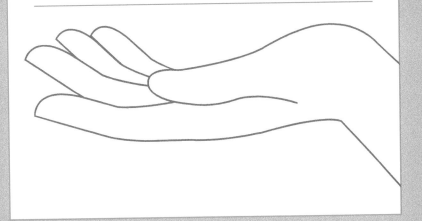

Doubt is not from God, for His Spirit lives within us, allowing us to set aside feelings of doubt and pick up faith. Discuss with your partner how you typically handle feelings of doubt. How can you encourage and remind each other that the Lord did not intend for us to carry this burden?

PARTNER 1: _____

_____

_____

_____

_____

_____

PARTNER 2: _____

_____

_____

_____

_____

_____

Difficult emotions can quickly become overwhelming. What makes you feel powerful, full of love, and in control? Get out a piece of paper and write down a few truths you can refer to when doubt or fear tries to take over. (Example: *The Lord's strength will encourage me.*)

PARTNER 1: _____

_____

_____

_____

_____

PARTNER 2: _____

_____

_____

_____

_____

Guided Prayer

Thank You, God, for going before me. For paving the way and allowing me to cling tightly to You in times when I feel lost, confused, or fearful. I am grateful that I serve a God who carries me through, when I feel unable to take another step on my own. Amen.

Week 16

The Lord will vindicate me; your love, Lord, endures forever—do not abandon the works of your hands.

—Psalm 138:8

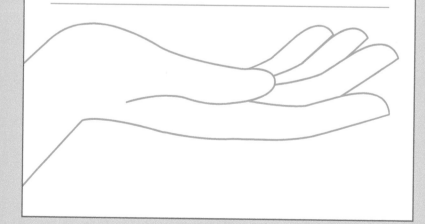

This verse reminds us that the Lord created us with a purpose. When He worked you into creation, He already had a purpose specifically set out for you. Discuss what you believe to be your purpose and how you can encourage each other to seek out your calling. How can you use your purpose to improve your relationship?

PARTNER 1: _____

_____

_____

_____

_____

_____

PARTNER 2: _____

_____

_____

_____

_____

_____

_____

Not every moment is grand or exciting. Just as the Lord takes His time in preparing us for what He has for us, we can learn to find joy in the little, everyday moments. Think of a few mundane tasks, and consider how, together, you could make them more enjoyable. Be as silly and creative as you'd like in your brainstorming.

PARTNER 1: _____

_____

_____

_____

_____

PARTNER 2: _____

_____

_____

_____

Action of the Week
Don't let the workload of your week interfere with making time to grow closer to each other (and the Lord). Plan a little outing together this week. Setting aside time to invest in your relationship helps foster growth, love, and intimacy.

Week 17

The tongue has the power of life and death, and those who love it will eat its fruit.

—Proverbs 18:21

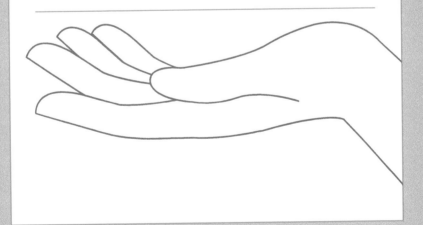

The words we say have more weight than we realize, as we are reminded in this verse. If we are gentle with our words, using them to speak life within our relationship, then we will see great benefits. What does it mean to you to speak life to your partner?

PARTNER 1: _____

_____

_____

_____

_____

_____

_____

PARTNER 2: _____

_____

_____

_____

_____

_____

Think about a time when someone else's words impacted your mood, in a good or bad way. How would you rate your ability to choose words carefully? How can you be cautious of your partner's feelings, especially when what you have to say may not be what they want to hear?

PARTNER 1: _____

_____

_____

_____

_____

PARTNER 2: _____

_____

_____

_____

_____

Guided Prayer

Lord, teach me how to use my words to uplift and encourage those with whom I come into contact—especially my partner. Use me to bring light into the lives of others with the words I speak. Please guide me in serving You with this gift. Amen.

Week 18

Whoever is patient has great understanding, but one who is quick-tempered displays folly.

—Proverbs 14:29

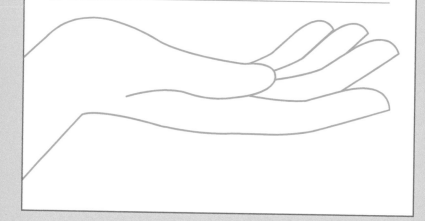

Sometimes our initial reaction to a situation may be anger, but we don't have to give in to that feeling. Learning to slow down and take a moment to register our emotions can help us choose a different path. Discuss with your partner how you can each learn to sit with your emotions before reacting with negativity.

PARTNER 1: _____

_____

_____

_____

_____

_____

PARTNER 2: _____

_____

_____

_____

_____

_____

Have you ever found yourself in a disagreement and felt like you must get to the bottom of it and solve the situation immediately? Sometimes it's better for both sides to step away to calm down, think through emotions, and come back to each other with a level head. How do you feel doing this might help?

PARTNER 1: _____

_____

_____

_____

_____

PARTNER 2: _____

_____

_____

_____

_____

Action of the Week

Setting aside time to be playful with your partner allows for shared lightheartedness. This can help the relationship flourish and still feel "new" regardless of how long you've been together. Pick a night this week to play one of your favorite games.

Week 19

*Anger is cruel and fury overwhelming,
but who can stand before jealousy?*

—Proverbs 27:4

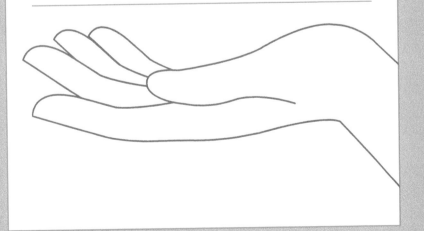

Jealousy has the ability to steal harmony and peace from a relationship. Has jealousy occurred in your relationship? If so, why do you think jealousy has been an issue? How can you combat feelings of jealousy, allay each other's insecurities, and be on the same page with your partner?

PARTNER 1: _____

_____

_____

_____

_____

_____

PARTNER 2: _____

_____

_____

_____

_____

_____

It's important to respect boundaries and ultimately to trust each other. Discuss together how you can make each other feel secure in your relationship. Reflect and come up with three compliments—things that shine a light on what you love about each other.

PARTNER 1: _____

_____

_____

_____

_____

PARTNER 2: _____

_____

_____

_____

_____

Guided Prayer

Lord, I pray that You would cover our relationship with Your presence. Allow us to walk with You and experience the good things that You have in store. By inviting You into the center of our relationship, we hope to grow closer to each other while honoring You. Amen.

Week 20

But grow in the grace and knowledge of our Lord and Savior Jesus Christ. To Him be glory both now and forever! Amen.

—2 Peter 3:18

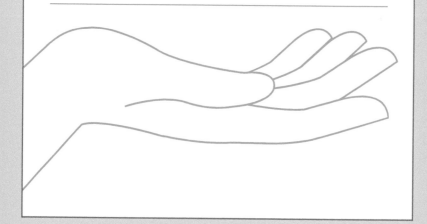

To foster a relationship that honors Jesus, we can make Him a part of our daily experience. We can also be a fountain of encouragement to our partner in growing their faith. There are many ways that we can be a stepping-stone in our partner's faith journey. How can you encourage each other to seek Jesus in daily life?

PARTNER 1: _____

_____

_____

_____

_____

_____

PARTNER 2: _____

_____

_____

_____

_____

_____

Even the greatest believers have room to continue to grow in their faith. There is always more we can learn about Jesus, who He is, and what His heart is about. Discuss ways that you and your partner can work to continue your faith walk. (One example is what you are doing right now by taking part in this journaling process.)

PARTNER 1: _____

_____

_____

_____

_____

PARTNER 2: _____

_____

_____

_____

_____

Action of the Week
Choose one activity this week that you will take part in together to spend time serving Jesus in a way that you normally don't. Maybe this means attending a midweek service at church, volunteering in the community, or reaching out to a neighbor in need.

Week 21

But when you pray, go into your room, close the door and pray to your Father, who is unseen. Then your Father, who sees what is done in secret, will reward you.

—Matthew 6:6

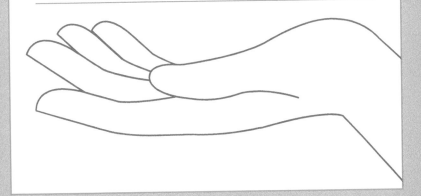

As important as it may be to attend church or Bible study groups, there is special significance to seeking Jesus in private. Those solo, prayer-filled moments spent behind closed doors reap good things. Why do you think it's so important to seek Him and spend time with Him when no one else sees?

PARTNER 1: _____

_____

_____

_____

_____

_____

PARTNER 2: _____

_____

_____

_____

_____

_____

Spending one-on-one time with the Lord allows your personal relationship with Him to go even deeper. Sometimes it may feel boring to sit in your room in prayer. Maybe you feel you have too much else to do. How can you encourage yourselves, and each other, to prioritize one-on-one time with the Lord?

PARTNER 1: _____

_____

_____

_____

_____

PARTNER 2: _____

_____

_____

_____

_____

Guided Prayer

Lord, I am grateful that Your presence is readily available to me. I don't have to be in church or sitting with my Bible open to spend time with You. You follow me throughout my day, allowing me to include You in my daily tasks. I will not take for granted my ability to seek You and invite You in right where I'm at. Amen.

Week 22

I have hidden your word in my heart that I might not sin against you.

—Psalm 119:11

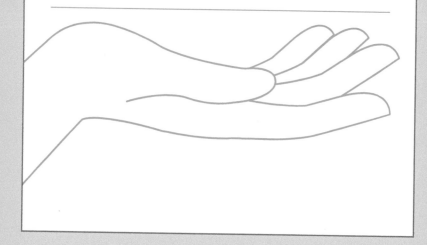

The more we read Scripture and discuss our faith with others, the more we can understand and incorporate it into our daily lives. How can you and your partner choose to live in accordance with your values? How can you do this together with love and understanding, being cautious to avoid judgment when one of you falls short?

PARTNER 1: _____

_____

_____

_____

_____

_____

PARTNER 2: _____

_____

_____

_____

_____

_____

Scripture presents us with a powerful tool. It familiarizes us with God's Word, increases our understanding of who He is, and allows us to grow closer to Him. How can you practice memorizing Scripture? How do you believe that memorizing Scripture will equip you in certain situations, such as when facing anxiety or having doubts?

PARTNER 1: _____

_____

_____

_____

_____

PARTNER 2: _____

_____

_____

_____

_____

Action of the Week

Take some time to memorize Scripture. Choose a verse that is meaningful to you both together, or each a different one. Write the verse down and hang it somewhere you'll see it often, such as the bathroom mirror. Each time you see it, read it aloud, until you can repeat it to each other without having to look.

Week 23

*I sought the Lord, and He answered me;
He delivered me from all my fears.*

—Psalm 34:4

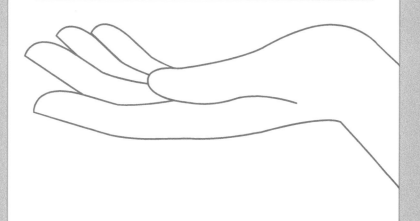

When we find ourselves in a place of fear, we can seek Jesus right in that moment. He's ready for our call no matter where we are or what's happening around us. What do you typically do in the face of fear? How does your partner help you stand up to feelings of fear? How can they help even more? Brainstorm and share your thoughts.

PARTNER 1: _____

_____

_____

_____

_____

_____

_____

PARTNER 2: _____

_____

_____

_____

_____

_____

_____

The easiest thing we can do in times of fear is pray. Even when we lack the words to string together, simply whispering "Jesus" can diminish fear and replace it with hope. When your partner experiences fear with something they are walking through, how do you encourage them? How can you remind them of Jesus's presence?

PARTNER 1: _____

_____

_____

_____

_____

PARTNER 2: _____

_____

_____

_____

_____

Guided Prayer
Thank you, Jesus, for always hearing my prayers. I find peace in knowing that no prayer goes unheard, and that You know what I am about to say before I even say it. Knowing that I can speak directly to You is incredible, and I will not underestimate the power of prayer. Amen.

Week 24

Two are better than one, because they have a good return for their labor: If either of them falls down, one can help the other up. But pity anyone who falls and has no one to help them up.

—Ecclesiastes 4:9–10

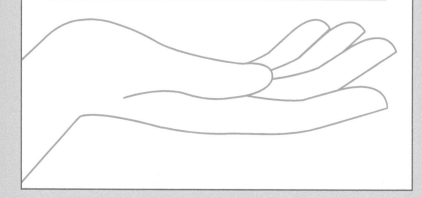

Whether you and your partner are in a long-term relationship, engaged, or married, you have someone to encourage you, support you, cry with you—how special is that? What's something your partner does for you that you really appreciate? Why does this gesture resonate with you?

PARTNER 1: _____

_____

_____

_____

_____

_____

PARTNER 2: _____

_____

_____

_____

_____

_____

This verse reminds us that having a partner means having someone to pick us up if we fall. This can be a powerful tool in relation to our walk with the Lord. If one of you is struggling in your faith or with something you're facing, you can point each other back to the Lord. Discuss with your partner how they play, or can play, a part in keeping you on track with your faith.

PARTNER 1: _____

_____

_____

_____

PARTNER 2: _____

_____

_____

_____

Action of the Week
Having a partner to "do life with" is such a blessing. Carve out time this week to step away from duties and simply enjoy having your special someone to go through life with. Sit for a special meal and chat, watch a movie together under a blanket, or play a card game.

Week 25

But a man who commits adultery has no sense; whoever does so destroys himself.

—Proverbs 6:32

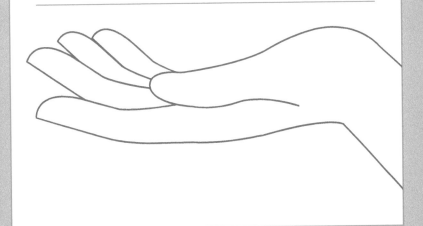

When we choose a partner, we are choosing to be faithful to them. We are promising to be honest with them and not betray their trust. Being unfaithful in a relationship is damaging to our partner and our relationship, but also to the Lord. Besides a physical relationship, how is it possible to be unfaithful to your partner?

PARTNER 1: _____

_____

_____

_____

_____

_____

PARTNER 2: _____

_____

_____

_____

_____

_____

When you choose to go through life with someone, it is up to you to remain faithful to your partner. How can you honor and demonstrate your commitment to each other? Have fun discussing ways that you can show a little extra love to each other and remind your partner that your heart is set on them.

PARTNER 1: _____

_____

_____

_____

_____

PARTNER 2: _____

_____

_____

_____

_____

Guided Prayer
Jesus, I am grateful that You have laid out for me the things I need to follow. You have given me the tools to walk in stride with You and have integrity. I pray that I would only make decisions that please You. Amen.

Week 26

*Be completely humble and gentle;
be patient bearing with one another in
love. Make every effort to keep the unity
of the Spirit through the bond of peace.*

—Ephesians 4:2–3

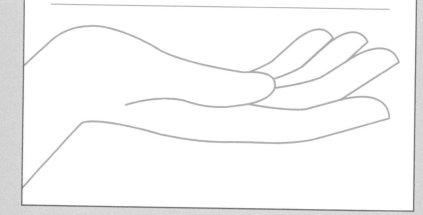

As time goes on in a relationship, we may get annoyed by things that didn't bother us before. This verse reminds us not only to be gentle with each other but also to always lead with love. Each partner brings different strengths and gifts to the table. How can you be intentional in using your God-given gifts to lead with love in your relationship?

PARTNER 1: _____

_____

_____

_____

_____

_____

PARTNER 2: _____

_____

_____

_____

_____

_____

In this world that's often filled with strife and uncertainty, it can bring peace and comfort to know we can turn inward to our partner to give and receive love, patience, and understanding. This brings us closer to the Lord and each other, and makes life easier. Think of areas within your relationship where you can find ways to further increase your unity with each other.

PARTNER 1: _____

_____

_____

_____

_____

PARTNER 2: _____

_____

_____

_____

Guided Prayer
Lord, I pray that I will be a blessing to my partner. I want to uplift and encourage my partner, allowing us to feel closer to each other and to You. Help me improve in areas where I need a bit more guidance to be my best self for them. Amen.

Week 27

Each of you should use whatever gift you have received to serve others, as faithful stewards of God's grace in its various forms.

—1 Peter 4:10

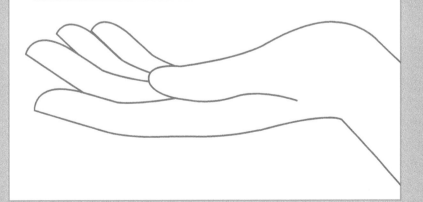

When God created you, He gave you specific gifts and talents. They are entirely personalized to you, and how you decide to use these gifts is up to you. Discuss with your partner some of the gifts you believe the Lord weaved into them at creation. Write them down, and then write what you believe your own special gifts to be.

PARTNER 1: _____

_____

_____

_____

_____

_____

PARTNER 2: _____

_____

_____

_____

_____

_____

The gifts God gave you can be used to glorify Him and His Kingdom. They are also designed to be used to serve others, as this verse tells us. By serving others, we are also serving the Lord. How can you use your gifts to serve your partner and your relationship?

PARTNER 1: _____

_____

_____

_____

_____

PARTNER 2: _____

_____

_____

_____

_____

Action of the Week
Be intentional this week in thinking of how you can better serve your partner. These don't have to be grand gestures; for example, bringing them coffee in bed, running an errand so they don't have to, or watching their favorite show with them.

Week 28

Put your outdoor work in order and get your fields ready; after that, build your house.

—Proverbs 24:27

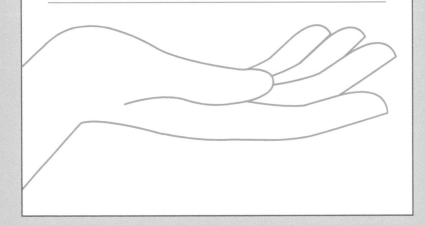

A house requires a good foundation, just like a healthy, lasting Christian relationship requires the Lord as its rock. Trust, comfort, and understanding are all pieces of a relationship that take time to establish. Discuss with your partner some of these key things and how they have come into fruition in your relationship.

PARTNER 1: _____

_____

_____

_____

_____

_____

PARTNER 2: _____

_____

_____

_____

_____

_____

You and your partner know the ins and outs of your relationship better than anyone, besides the Lord. A relationship is all about learning and growing together, strengthening as you foster its development. What areas in your relationship have you strengthened over time? Which could you work on to create a sturdier, more solid foundation?

PARTNER 1: _____

_____

_____

_____

_____

PARTNER 2: _____

_____

_____

_____

_____

Guided Prayer

Lord, I'm grateful that You are the foundation within our relationship. Without You as the center, the main building block, we would stumble. We desire to continue to build and learn from You. Show us ways to improve or grow, guiding us to be the best partner we can be to each other. Amen.

Week 29

Do not conform to the pattern of this world, but be transformed by the renewing of your mind. Then you will be able to test and approve what God's will is—His good, pleasing and perfect will.

—Romans 12:2

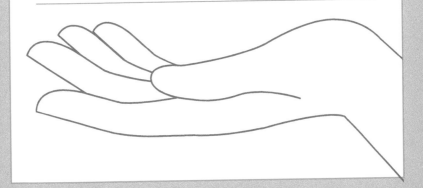

There are plenty of people who will tell you what makes a relationship work and what you need to do to keep your partner happy. But there's a difference between what the world says and what the Lord says. Discuss with your partner some of these differences.

PARTNER 1: _____

_____

_____

_____

_____

_____

PARTNER 2: _____

_____

_____

_____

_____

_____

Sometimes relationships fall into a pattern of disagreements, feelings of inadequacy, or loneliness. A "renewing of our mind" can help shift us into patterns of love, communication, growth, and intimacy. Take a step back and evaluate your recent exchanges, thoughts, and actions. How can pausing first to take things to the Lord renew your mind and benefit your relationship?

PARTNER 1: _____

_____

_____

_____

_____

PARTNER 2: _____

_____

_____

_____

_____

Action of the Week

Spending quality time together is very important. It can be as simple as a meaningful conversation without any distractions. Take a walk together and chat about your week. What were the highs and lows? Don't be afraid to let the conversation flow to deeper topics.

Week 30

Carry each other's burdens, and in this way you will fulfill the law of Christ.

—Galatians 6:2

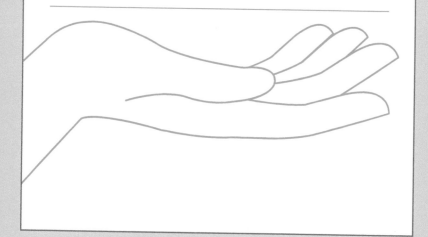

Even when following the Lord, we will still have burdens to carry and hardships to walk through. But by living for Jesus, following Jesus, we have all that we need to face these difficult trials. Discuss with your partner how Jesus helps you through.

PARTNER 1: _____

_____

_____

_____

_____

_____

PARTNER 2: _____

_____

_____

_____

_____

_____

God put us together to share life with. This includes helping carry each other's burdens to make them easier to bear. Doing so means pointing each other back to Jesus when needed. It means sitting with them in sorrow when they experience heartache. How can you do that within your relationship? How do you do that already?

PARTNER 1: _____

_____

_____

_____

_____

PARTNER 2: _____

_____

_____

_____

_____

Action of the Week
It's important (and fun) to sit back and reflect on your relationship—the things you've experienced together, the ways you've grown, and everything in between. Write each other a note that you'll open at the end of the week. Include some of your favorite memories and why you appreciate each other.

Week 31

A new command I give you: Love one another. As I have loved you, so you must love one another.

—John 13:34

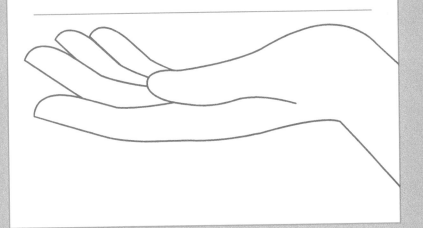

As a relationship grows, it's natural to learn more about your partner. You learn how they like to be shown love and affection as well as reciprocate that love to you. Maybe their love language is words of affirmation, whereas yours is touch. Are you aware of your partner's love language? What do you see as each other's love language?

PARTNER 1: _____

_____

_____

_____

_____

_____

PARTNER 2: _____

_____

_____

_____

_____

_____

By showing love to others, we are also following God's Word, as loving others is one of His commandments to us. It's important for us as followers of Christ to try to love like Jesus does, by showing it through our actions in addition to holding it in our hearts. How can you improve the way you love your partner and others?

PARTNER 1: _____

_____

_____

_____

_____

PARTNER 2: _____

_____

_____

_____

_____

Guided Prayer
Lord, I aspire to love like You do. Love is the most powerful thing You have given to us, and I want to live that out in my day-to-day life. Teach me how to love others to the best of my ability, allowing this to reflect the love You pour out to us daily. Amen.

Week 32

But he said to me, "My grace is sufficient for you, for my power is made perfect in weakness." Therefore I will boast all the more gladly about my weaknesses, so that Christ's power may rest on me.

—2 Corinthians 12:9

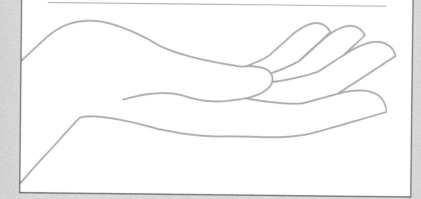

Think about a time when you felt weak or lost in a situation. Did you have confidence in knowing that the Lord's strength covers your weakness? Discuss with your partner what it means to rely on the Lord's strength and how you can do this when challenges arise.

PARTNER 1: _____

_____

_____

_____

_____

_____

PARTNER 2: _____

_____

_____

_____

_____

_____

In this verse, we are told that God's grace is enough for us. As Christians, we may hear this phrase often. The grace we receive from the Lord allows us to be mindful in how we approach different situations. Discuss how you can use God's grace to handle problems both big and small, inside and outside your relationship.

PARTNER 1: _____

_____

_____

_____

_____

PARTNER 2: _____

_____

_____

_____

Action of the Week
What's something the two of you have always wanted to try? This week, explore that activity, big or small. Enjoy the fun of trying something new together and allow yourselves to grow closer as you get to laugh at the need for God's grace when trying something outside your comfort zone. Don't be ashamed to make mistakes and learn; that's what trying something new is all about.

Week 33

I praise you because I am fearfully and wonderfully made; your works are wonderful, I know that full well.

—Psalm 139:14

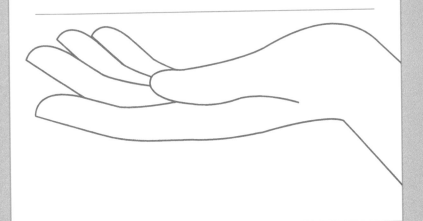

Nothing the Lord created was a mistake. It is important that we as Christians see ourselves as being God's handiwork, wonderfully made with purpose. Loving who God made us to be is something we can live out each day. How can you choose to love who you are? What does loving yourself and who God made you to be look like to you, as an individual and a partner?

PARTNER 1: _____

_____

_____

_____

_____

_____

PARTNER 2: _____

_____

_____

_____

_____

_____

Sometimes we may feel discouraged or down on ourselves. Our shortcomings don't reflect the worth that we hold—our worth is in God. How can you be supportive and encourage your partner to love themselves? What can you do to remind them of the worth they have in the Lord?

PARTNER 1: _____

_____

_____

_____

_____

PARTNER 2: _____

_____

_____

_____

_____

Guided Prayer
Lord, I pray that I would see myself the way that You see me. You created me intentionally, without mistake. Nothing that I do could diminish the worth You instilled in me from Creation. I'm so grateful to be loved by such a loving Father. Amen.

Week 34

Do not let any unwholesome talk come out of your mouths, but only what is helpful for building others up according to their needs, that it may benefit those who listen.

—Ephesians 4:29

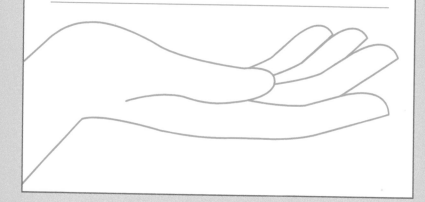

Sometimes you may feel the urge to vent to others about your relationship. Before you do this, pause and take a step back. It's better to first take it to God and then reconcile directly when tensions have lightened. What strengths do the two of you have when it comes to healthy communication? How could you improve?

PARTNER 1: _____

_____

_____

_____

_____

_____

PARTNER 2: _____

_____

_____

_____

_____

_____

It's up to us to support our partner and to have their back. A big way that we can protect them is with our words. Have fun with your words, focusing on what you love about each other. Look your partner in the eyes and tell them some things you admire about them.

PARTNER 1: _____

_____

_____

_____

_____

PARTNER 2: _____

_____

_____

_____

_____

Action of the Week
In the midst of a disagreement or argument is the perfect time to practice handling your emotions. Practice uplifting your partner and remaining positive toward them even when it may feel difficult. This week, tell your partner what you love about them and why you feel it is a blessing to learn and grow with each other. See how this experience feels for you.

Week 35

"For I know the plans I have for you,"
declares the Lord, "plans to prosper
you and not to harm you, plans to give
you hope and a future."

—Jeremiah 29:11

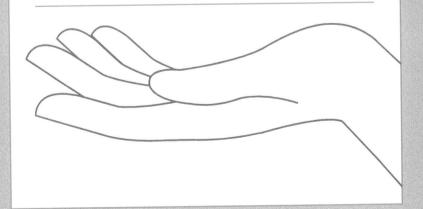

From the moment the Lord created you, He had a purpose for your life. He knew the people you would meet and the paths you would take. Discuss with your partner a time in your life when you didn't know where God was leading you or what the outcome would be. Reflect also on how you met and consider how God had a hand in that.

PARTNER 1: _____

_____

_____

_____

_____

_____

PARTNER 2: _____

_____

_____

_____

_____

_____

_____

This verse tells us that the Lord has good plans for us, plans for success and hope. How do you think this is playing out in your relationship? What do you think your future together holds?

PARTNER 1: _____

_____

_____

_____

_____

PARTNER 2: _____

_____

_____

_____

_____

Guided Prayer
Lord, I desire to walk in the purpose that You have for my life. I know that You have good things in store for me and us and that we are on the journey You have set out for our life together. Teach us how to be joyful through the hard parts and keep our eyes on You, knowing that Your plans for us are good. Amen.

Week 36

If we confess our sins, he is faithful and just and will forgive us our sins and purify us from all unrighteousness.

—1 John 1:9

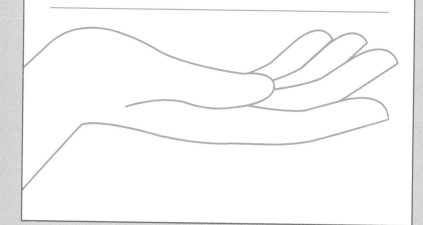

There is nothing too big or too ugly for God to forgive. Sometimes we even need forgiveness for our attitude, how we've been treating our partner, or neglecting time that should be spent with Jesus. How can you reflect and together ask for God's mercy, if needed?

PARTNER 1: _____

_____

_____

_____

_____

_____

PARTNER 2: _____

_____

_____

_____

_____

_____

Just as we ask forgiveness from the Lord, it's important to ask for forgiveness from our partner. It can be difficult to admit when we're at fault or should've gone about something differently. How would you rate your ability to acknowledge when you're wrong and apologize? How can you get better at this?

PARTNER 1: _____

_____

_____

_____

_____

PARTNER 2: _____

_____

_____

_____

_____

Guided Prayer
Thank you, Lord, for not judging me when I fall short. You always welcome me in with open arms, ready to forgive my wrongs. Allow me to do the same in being gracious with forgiving my partner and quick to ask for forgiveness. Amen.

Week 37

If one part suffers, every part suffers with it; if one part is honored, every part rejoices with it.

—1 Corinthians 12:26

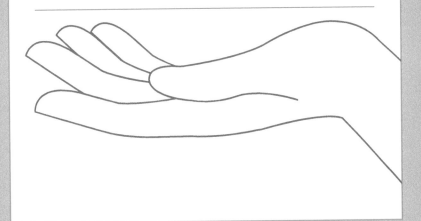

You and your partner are on the same team, and working together is what makes all of the pieces work. One can't give 20 percent while the other gives 80 percent and expect the relationship to roll smoothly. How can you both be intentional in putting in the necessary effort to make your relationship flourish?

PARTNER 1: _____

_____

_____

_____

_____

_____

PARTNER 2: _____

_____

_____

_____

_____

_____

Did you know that the longer you are in a relationship, the more you begin to act like each other? Your emotions become entwined with each other's, causing you to feel happy when they are happy and sad when they're sad. Tell your partner in what ways you believe that a piece of your heart belongs to them and how, in turn, this allows you to feel what they feel.

PARTNER 1: _____

_____

_____

_____

_____

PARTNER 2: _____

_____

_____

_____

_____

Action of the Week
Making time to have fun and enjoy each other's company is fuel for your relationship. Cut up slips of paper and write down as many date ideas as you can think of. Get creative; they don't need to involve leaving the house or spending money. Put these date ideas into a jar and make a promise to pull one out weekly.

Week 38

He will yet fill your mouth with laughter and your lips with shouts of joy.

—Job 8:21

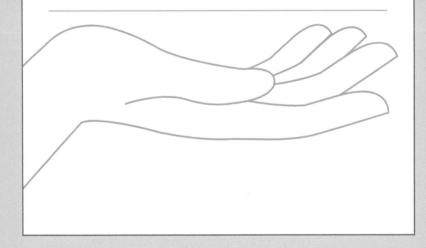

Joy does not depend on circumstances—we can find joy anytime. What are some ways you can be more intentional in choosing joy, knowing that true joy comes from Christ? How can you shift your perspective to one of greater joy?

PARTNER 1: _____

_____

_____

_____

_____

_____

PARTNER 2: _____

_____

_____

_____

_____

_____

Discuss with your partner what it is that drew you to them and what draws you to them now. How has what draws you to each other changed over time? Have fun seeing the ways in which your attraction to each other has grown, shifted, and expanded.

PARTNER 1: _____

_____

_____

_____

_____

PARTNER 2: _____

_____

_____

_____

Action of the Week
Think back to one of the first dates you and your partner went on. Was it going to the movies, dinner, or an adventure? Those first dates paved the way to your relationship and played a part in getting you to where you are now. Try your best to remake that date, whether that be going back to the same place or creating a similar experience.

Week 39

Greater love has no one than this: to lay down one's life for one's friends.

—John 15:13

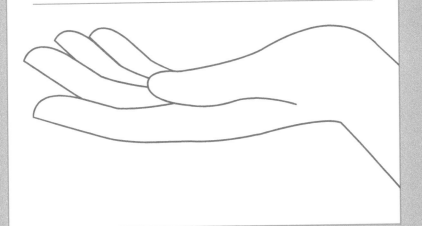

Most people believe their significant other is also their best friend—is this true for the two of you? Do you give your partner the same or greater respect, understanding, and effort that you give your friends? Why or why not? How can you be a better friend to your partner? What does the ideal friendship look like to each of you?

PARTNER 1: _____

_____

_____

_____

_____

_____

PARTNER 2: _____

_____

_____

_____

_____

_____

This verse says there is no love greater than to lay your life down for a friend. This reflects in our heart posture toward our life partner—what we're willing to do for them and our attitude in doing so. What are some examples of things you do or have done for your partner (or that they've done for you) that reflect this verse? Talk about how you feel protective of them.

PARTNER 1: _____

_____

_____

_____

_____

PARTNER 2: _____

_____

_____

_____

_____

Guided Prayer
Lord, help me be the friend that my partner needs. Give me a heart of service and an attitude of joy and willingness. Quell any feelings of selfishness that want to creep in, and guide us in living out this great love of laying down our wants in order to joyfully serve each other. Amen.

Week 40

Pride brings a person low, but the lowly in spirit gain honor.

—Proverbs 29:23

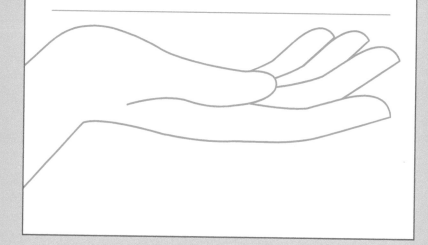

Pride takes the focus off God and puts it onto ourselves. If we aren't careful, pride can become an ugly giant within our relationship, resulting in an "I do it better" or "I know more" type of attitude. Is pride ever an issue for you? How can you combat pride within your relationship? What does that look like to you personally?

PARTNER 1: _____

_____

_____

_____

_____

_____

PARTNER 2: _____

_____

_____

_____

_____

_____

When we boast of or flaunt our accomplishments, sometimes we forget who it was that got us there in the first place. Being humble serves God, and it feels good. Discuss with your partner how you can have a humble spirit and live that out in your daily life.

PARTNER 1: _____

_____

_____

_____

_____

PARTNER 2: _____

_____

_____

_____

_____

Guided Prayer

Lord, keep my eyes and my heart focused on You. Give me a spirit that is humble, one that honors You above all else. I am aware of Your hand in every detail, in every aspect of my life, and I never want to place the glory elsewhere. Thank You for the blessings You have given me. Your goodness does not go unnoticed. Amen.

Week 41

Since, then, you have been raised with Christ, set your hearts on things above, where Christ is, seated at the right hand of God.

—Colossians 3:1

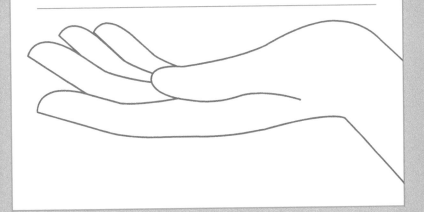

As followers of Christ, we're instructed to keep our focus on things of Heaven, not to follow trends or hop onto whatever worldly thing or activity is popular at the time. How can you avoid following pop culture and keep your eyes on Jesus? How can you encourage each other in this?

PARTNER 1: _____

_____

_____

_____

_____

_____

PARTNER 2: _____

_____

_____

_____

_____

_____

By fixing our eyes on Jesus, we put good things on the forefront of our hearts. This allows us to be a better partner and to be more patient, loving, and understanding. Take a moment and reflect on how the way you serve your partner can directly relate back to Jesus. How does your partner reflect Jesus in the way that they love you?

PARTNER 1: _____

_____

_____

_____

_____

PARTNER 2: _____

_____

_____

_____

_____

Action of the Week
To keep the focus on Jesus, find a way that you can give back to the community this week, such as volunteering at church or at a local shelter or food bank. Talk together about the experience.

Week 42

You did not choose me, but I chose you and appointed you so that you might go and bear fruit—fruit that will last—and so that whatever you ask in my name the Father will give you.

—John 15:16

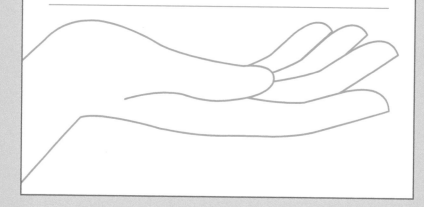

By following Christ, we put the nine fruits of the Spirit within our reach. The fruits of the Spirit include love, joy, peace, patience, kindness, generosity, faithfulness, gentleness, and self-control (Galatians 5:22). How do you think these fruits appear in your relationship with each other? What fruits do you wish to bear more readily, and how?

PARTNER 1: _____

_____

_____

_____

_____

_____

_____

PARTNER 2: _____

_____

_____

_____

_____

_____

_____

The Lord chose us and continues choosing us, and it is up to us to continue to choose Him back by leaning into Him and bearing fruit that will last. Even beyond your relationship, what fruits are you inspired to bear in your community, and how can you do this?

PARTNER 1: _____

_____

_____

_____

_____

PARTNER 2: _____

_____

_____

_____

Guided Prayer
Thank You, Jesus, that You are continually chasing after me. You desire closeness with me and do not want me to walk through life separately from You. Help me to abide in You and Your Word and lean into Your will for my life. Amen.

Week 43

Marriage should be honored by all, and the marriage bed kept pure.

—Hebrews 13:4

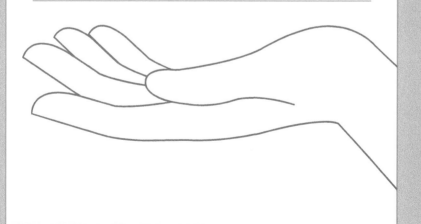

Whether you're dating, in a long-term relationship, engaged, or married, it is vital to have boundaries regarding intimacy. God designed sex to be beneficial, healthy, and comfortable. Discuss with your partner what forms of intimacy allow for the two of you to feel close and connected. Talk about how you'd like to enhance your intimacy.

PARTNER 1: _____

_____

_____

_____

_____

_____

PARTNER 2: _____

_____

_____

_____

_____

_____

How you express love to your partner is unique to each individual and the relationship as a whole. You may find that your partner likes holding hands in public, whereas you always make the effort to give a goodbye kiss before leaving. Discuss with your partner how you can grow into new levels of closeness and love that will honor your commitment to each other.

PARTNER 1: _____

_____

_____

_____

_____

PARTNER 2: _____

_____

_____

_____

_____

Action of the Week
In the midst of busy schedules, it's important to make time for fun with each other. This week, allow yourselves to completely unplug—no phones, no TV—and go explore a path you've never before experienced.

Week 44

Then you will call on me and come and pray to me, and I will listen to you.

—Jeremiah 29:12

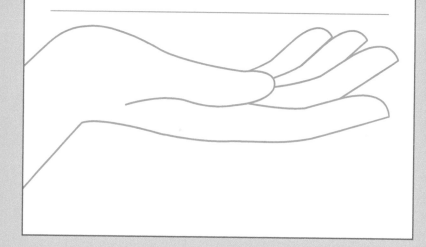

We don't need to limit prayer to times of desperation. We can simply have a conversation with the Lord, spending quality time in His presence by chatting, celebrating, or expressing thankfulness. In what ways can you enhance your prayer life? How could changing the way you pray benefit you? Is this something you can do together? How?

PARTNER 1: _____

_____

_____

_____

_____

_____

PARTNER 2: _____

_____

_____

_____

_____

_____

The constant availability of Jesus through prayer is a priceless tool, a blessing that sometimes gets overlooked. Prayer needs not be limited to a specific time of day or topic. Discuss with your partner how praying for and with each other can strengthen your relationship. How can you use prayer individually and together to increase the "power of prayer"?

PARTNER 1: _____

_____

_____

_____

_____

PARTNER 2: _____

_____

_____

_____

_____

Action of the Week
The Lord wants to hear from us throughout our day. Praying over your partner and relationship is a great way to keep God at the center. Making prayer a common ritual within your relationship will allow for increased comfort, trust, and peace. Take turns saying a prayer for each other and over your relationship.

Week 45

Love is patient, love is kind. It does not envy, it does not boast, it is not proud. It does not dishonor others, it is not self-seeking, it is not easily angered, it keeps no record of wrongs.

—1 Corinthians 13:4–5

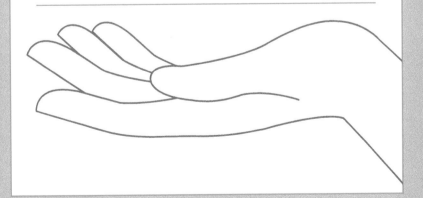

These verses direct us on what love should look like, giving us a blueprint of how to love well. Reflect on a specific time within your relationship where love was particularly patient and kind. What features within your relationship are proof that these characteristics are present in your love with each other?

PARTNER 1: _____

_____

_____

_____

_____

_____

PARTNER 2: _____

_____

_____

_____

_____

_____

We are human—we all trip now and then. Think about times when your expressions to your partner did not measure up to the way the Bible describes love. In what ways did you fall short? What did you learn from this? Going forward, how can you be mindful of loving your partner in the truest sense of love?

PARTNER 1: _____

_____

_____

_____

_____

PARTNER 2: _____

_____

_____

_____

_____

Guided Prayer

Lord, I am thankful that You have shown me what perfect love looks like. Even when I do not feel I deserve it, Your love washes over me and holds no judgment. Allow me to become better at putting my needs to the side as I learn to love fully, without restriction. Teach me to love my partner in the way that You love me. Amen.

Week 46

Consider it pure joy, my brothers and sisters, whenever you face trials of many kinds, because you know that the testing of your faith produces perseverance.

—James 1:2–3

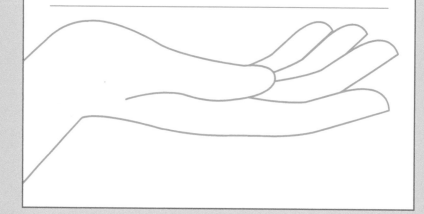

Choosing to live a life chasing after the Lord does not mean that you won't have to face difficult seasons. But in living for Jesus, you already have all you need to overcome any obstacle. Think of an obstacle you faced together in the past. Looking back, how do you think God played a role in the outcome and your grace when facing the situation?

PARTNER 1: _____

_____

_____

_____

_____

_____

PARTNER 2: _____

_____

_____

_____

_____

_____

When we face hardship, we are not without God. He walks alongside us. This verse tells us that by facing such trials, our faith can be strengthened. How can you change the way you view difficult situations, knowing that it can be a time God meant for growth? Is there a situation you're dealing with that you can find strength in, knowing He is there for you? How?

PARTNER 1: _____

_____

_____

_____

_____

PARTNER 2: _____

_____

_____

_____

_____

Action of the Week

Set aside time this week to look at pictures or revisit stories from your earliest memories together. Reflect on both the joys and the challenges and how you've grown together through them.

Week 47

The Lord is not slow in keeping His promise, as some understand slowness. Instead, He is patient with you, not wanting anyone to perish, but everyone to come to repentance.

—2 Peter 3:9

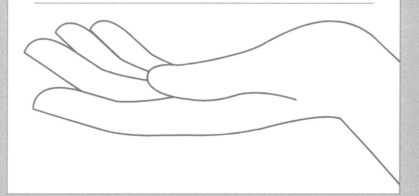

We sometimes forget that God works on His time, not ours. Do you struggle with wanting to see immediate results? How can you have confidence in knowing that God's plans for your life will come to fruition? Discuss a time when something that you had been praying for became reality.

PARTNER 1: _____

_____

_____

_____

_____

_____

_____

PARTNER 2: _____

_____

_____

_____

_____

_____

_____

Patience must be practiced; it doesn't necessarily come naturally. Think about how you react to your partner when they haven't done something you asked them to do. Do you immediately find yourself getting annoyed? What steps can you take to gain a more patient mindset?

PARTNER 1: _____

_____

_____

_____

_____

PARTNER 2: _____

_____

_____

_____

_____

Guided Prayer
Thank You, Jesus. I recognize that even when I do not see it, You are working on my behalf. In times of waiting, there is purpose to be found and praise to be given. Give me a patient heart, not only in my walk with You, but toward my partner. Amen.

Week 48

Do to others as you would have them do to you.

—Luke 6:31

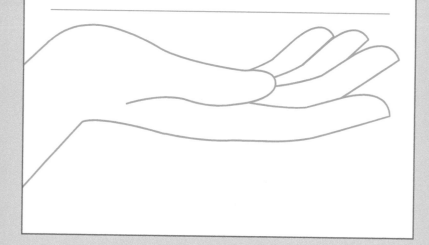

Ah, the Golden Rule, to treat others as we would like to be treated. Think of a time when you experienced the Golden Rule either being put to use or violated. What happened, and what reflections were you left with? Do you see eye to eye on the Golden Rule? How can the Golden Rule be a powerful tool in your relationship?

PARTNER 1: _____

_____

_____

_____

_____

_____

PARTNER 2: _____

_____

_____

_____

_____

_____

It can be easy to feed off the energy in the room—both positive and negative. Choosing to respond with gentleness, kindness, and understanding can be difficult when you're not receiving the same in return. Discuss with your partner how you can be mindful in treating each other and others with positivity, even when it feels hard.

PARTNER 1: _____

_____

_____

_____

_____

PARTNER 2: _____

_____

_____

_____

_____

Action of the Week

Putting forth kindness and compassion in all situations allows you to be more like Jesus. In return, it tends to leave you feeling good about yourself as well. This week, perform a random act of kindness. Perhaps help someone out with their task at work or buy a stranger's coffee. If you'd like, tell each other what happened, how it played out, and how it made you feel.

Week 49

Let us not become weary in doing good, for at the proper time we will reap a harvest if we do not give up.

—Galatians 6:9

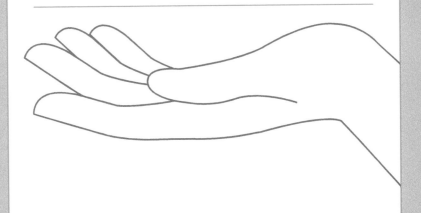

It can be exhausting to keep a joyful heart. But we are told to persevere, push forward, and continue doing good for the Lord, because nothing goes by unnoticed. Discuss a time when you felt discouraged and thought that doing good or putting in that work wasn't benefiting you. How did it resolve?

PARTNER 1: _____

_____

_____

_____

_____

_____

PARTNER 2: _____

_____

_____

_____

_____

_____

The reason we often allow ourselves to become weary in what we are working at is because we are not seeing the benefit or outcome we're hoping for. But that's the thing: God's plan is entirely different from ours, and for good reason. He knows all; we only see a small glimpse at a time. How can you keep yourself motivated to do good and walk by faith?

PARTNER 1: _____

_____

_____

_____

_____

PARTNER 2: _____

_____

_____

_____

_____

Guided Prayer

Lord, I am thankful that my hard work and perseverance do not pass You by unnoticed. The good that I am doing now is glorifying You and planting seeds that I will reap the benefits of later. Help me keep a joyful heart as I continue doing good to please You and bring glory to Your Name. Amen.

Week 50

Praise the Lord. Give thanks to the Lord, for He is good; His love endures forever.

—Psalm 106:1

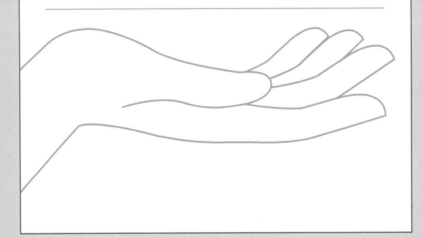

The simple action of praising Jesus throughout our day holds great influence on our feelings and emotions and how we will react when unexpected things are thrown our way. In what ways do you praise Jesus on a daily basis? What are things in your life that can remind you to praise Him?

PARTNER 1: _____

_____

_____

_____

_____

_____

PARTNER 2: _____

_____

_____

_____

_____

_____

It's a simple and common mistake to correlate how our lives are going with the level of God's goodness. But in reality, God's goodness never changes. It's the same on our best days as it is on our worst. Do you find yourself feeling negatively toward God when things aren't going the way you hoped? How can you remind yourself that God's goodness does not waver?

PARTNER 1: _____

_____

_____

_____

_____

PARTNER 2: _____

_____

_____

_____

_____

Action of the Week
Serving the Lord allows you to grow spiritually and be the light of Jesus for someone else. If you notice someone in need of a dose of kindness, step forward. By doing so, you're providing the blessing that they may not even have known they needed. This can be proof to others that God's love is present and alive, and that anyone is capable of being that vessel.

Week 51

By faith we understand that the universe was formed at God's command, so that what is seen was not made out of what was visible.

—Hebrews 11:3

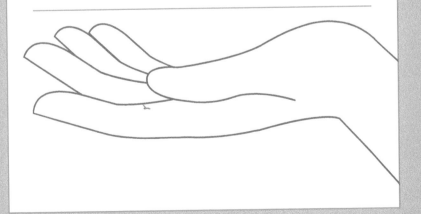

Our faith is based on what is unseen to us, although that does not change the realness of God and His love for us. We are cultivating a faith so strong that it does not require visible proof to know that Jesus is our protector, our strength, our hope. How can you work to exercise your faith to keep it strong? What can you add to or remove from your life to make this happen?

PARTNER 1: _____

_____

_____

_____

_____

_____

PARTNER 2: _____

_____

_____

_____

_____

_____

On the flip side, sometimes the fact that we cannot see God working on our behalf can be discouraging. We may wonder, "Does God see that I'm struggling?" Having a faith strong enough to silence these questions and doubts requires daily effort. Does your confidence in the Lord waver when you suffer? Discuss the areas in which your faith could use some improvement.

PARTNER 1: _____

_____

_____

_____

_____

PARTNER 2: _____

_____

_____

_____

Guided Prayer

I am grateful that my faith does not depend on my circumstances or my physical ability to see You. I have confidence in knowing that You are who You say You are, that Your goodness is overflowing, and Your hand is at work in my life. I will praise Your Name and give thanks. Amen.

Week 52

Do not be deceived: God cannot be mocked. A man reaps what he sows. Whoever sows to please their flesh, from the flesh will reap destruction; whoever sows to please the Spirit, from the Spirit will reap eternal life.

—Galatians 6:7–8

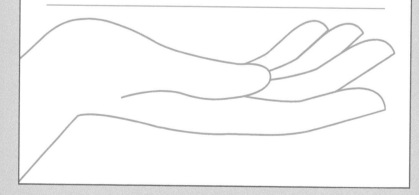

In a culture focused on personal success and growth, it's easy to feel that what you're doing isn't measuring up. You may ask, "Am I doing enough?" or "If I'm not making big moves, does what I'm doing really matter?" How can you avoid falling into this pattern of "me, me, me" and flip it to "Jesus, Jesus, Jesus"? How do you think this would change things for you?

PARTNER 1: _____

_____

_____

_____

_____

_____

PARTNER 2: _____

_____

_____

_____

_____

_____

No amount of status or luxury can provide the fullness of joy that Jesus gives. Discuss with your partner where you are putting your focus. Is it in temporary approval and satisfaction from things of this world, or in eternal life through Jesus? What does it look like to sow and reap things of the Spirit? How can you make this happen?

PARTNER 1: _____

_____

_____

_____

_____

PARTNER 2: _____

_____

_____

_____

_____

Guided Prayer

I put my focus on You, Lord. For what You openly offer to me daily is better than anything I could ever receive from this world. I desire to be Spirit-driven, pouring my heart and efforts into seeking You. Help me avoid the temptations that are all around me and keep my focus in the right place. Amen.

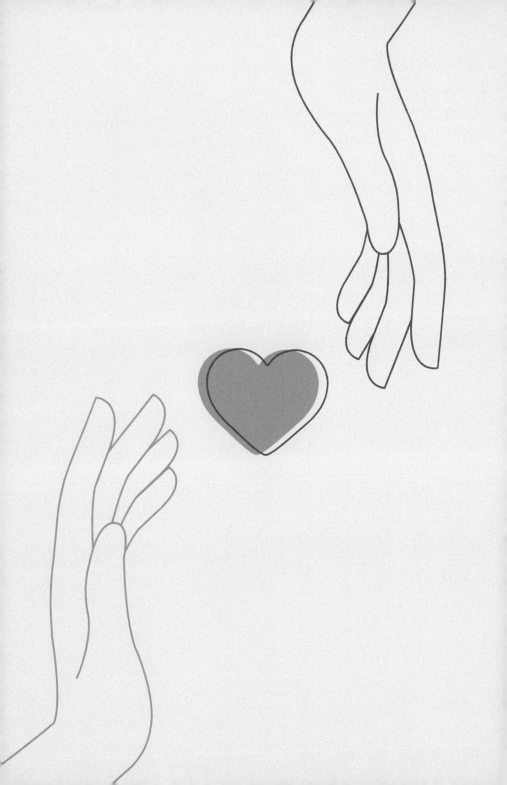

Continue to Nurture Your Love

Congratulations, it's time to celebrate! You have officially made it through an entire year—52 whole weeks of intentionally prioritizing your relationship with each other and your walk with Jesus. I pray that this journal allowed for growth within your personal relationship with Christ and each other and gave you a blueprint to continue seeking Jesus daily as a couple as you grow together in your relationship.

You've completed this book, but your journey's just beginning. Continue applying all you've learned to maintain a relationship that's a thriving, safe place you both can relish. Let your relationship be one that glorifies Jesus, putting Him first and watching the way that He guides your steps along the process. The degree to which you allow Jesus to shape your relationship personally and with each other relates to how you include Him into your daily interactions. Life that is lived with and for Jesus allows for fulfillment and joy. Let the reflections and practices you have worked on in these past 52 weeks carry you forward to a continued pattern of living a life that desires more of Him. Continue chasing after Jesus and the beautiful life that He has in store for the two of you.

ACKNOWLEDGMENTS

This devotional is dedicated to my sweet husband, Justin, who has been uplifting and encouraging me to achieve my dreams, no matter how big or small, since high school. Without your constant support, I would not be where I am today. The way you serve me and our family so selflessly directly reflects the goodness of Jesus each and every day. I love you!

ABOUT THE AUTHOR

Jenna Greer has an ongoing desire to chase after Jesus and live according to His greater purpose for her life. As a young stay-at-home mom from Minnesota, Jenna is constantly finding ways to connect with and encourage other believers in their walk with the Lord. You can keep up with her through her personal Instagram account, @jenmariegreer, where she shares her everyday life experiences as a mother, or through her other Instagram page dedicated to reaching women for Jesus, titled "Her with Purpose," where Jenna encourages women to seek Jesus and His purpose for their lives.